SHROPSHIRE RAILWAYS

MIKE HITCHES & JIM ROBERTS

SUTTON PUBLISHING LIMITED

Sutton Publishing Limited
Phoenix Mill · Far Thrupp · Stroud
Gloucestershire · GL5 2BU

First published 1996

Copyright © Mike Hitches & Jim Roberts,
1996

British Library Cataloguing in Publication Data
A catalogue record for this book is available from the
British Library.

ISBN 0-7509-1175-1

Typeset in 10/12 Perpetua.
Typesetting and origination by
Sutton Publishing Limited.
Printed in Great Britain by
Ebenezer Baylis, Worcester

To Sean

CONTENTS

The Severn Valley Railway is today the most famous section of railway in Shropshire, thanks to the marvellous efforts of the preservationists of the line between Bridgnorth and Kidderminster, Worcestershire. The section between Bridgnorth and Highley lies within Shropshire and sees many thousands of visitors a year ride on the railway and view the wonderful collection of ex-main line steam and diesel locomotives. The section between Shrewsbury and Bridgnorth ceased to exist in 1963 and the station at Ironbridge and Broseley was on that section. Seen here, in the last few years before closure, is ex-LMS Ivatt 2–6–2 tank locomotive no. 41209 with a local train to Shrewsbury.

INTRODUCTION

Shropshire is famous as the cradle of the Industrial Revolution, thanks to Abraham Darby, who first used coke instead of charcoal to smelt iron at his Coalbrookdale ironworks in 1709. He was also the first to cast iron in sand. The county was important in railway terms, being the first to lay iron rails, which replaced wooden ones, over a 2½ mile length of tramway serving an ironworks at Horsehay in 1767/8. The first cast-iron cylinders for steam locomotives were manufactured at Coalbrookdale.

Despite their importance in early railway development, the main lines that traversed Shropshire were intended for destinations elsewhere. The Shrewsbury & Birmingham (S&BR) and the Shrewsbury & Chester (S&CR) Railways are an example of this. The S&CR, opened in 1846, and the S&BR, which opened some three years later, met at the county town and were designed to link the industrial West Midlands with the major seaports on the River Mersey. In the meantime, the mighty London and North Western Railway (LNWR) had penetrated Shropshire. After taking control of the Shropshire Union Railways and Canal Company in 1847, its line between Stafford and the prosperous town of Wellington, where it met the S&BR, opened in 1849, just five months before the latter company completed its route between Shrewsbury and Wolverhampton.

Aware of the threat that the S&BR and S&CR made to LNWR monopoly in the north-west of England, Captain Mark Huish, the autocratic Managing Director of the Euston company, used his Shropshire Union Railways and Canal Company line to break the little Shrewsbury companies by undercutting fares between Wolverhampton and Wellington, despite the fact that his route was much longer than that of the S&BR. When this tactic did not work, Huish resorted to 'strong-arm' methods, preventing the S&BR from reaching Birmingham over the joint Stour Valley line from Wolverhampton, and physically threatening the S&CR at Chester when that company made an agreement with the S&BR for joint carriage of goods between Birkenhead and Birmingham which struck at the heart of LNWR traffic. Huish even went as far as setting up illegal Boards of Directors in his efforts to destroy these two very resilient little companies, such was the rough-and-tumble of Victorian railways. Such heavy-handed tactics by Huish seriously backfired on the Euston company because the two Shrewsbury companies sought friendship with the Great Western Railway (GWR), that broad gauge company which was loathed by Huish, and another one which he constantly threatened as its line approached the West Midlands. The GWR was very interested in having a route to reach potentially lucrative traffic from Merseyside, and to provide competition to the arrogant LNWR, even though its line had not yet even reached Birmingham. Thus, the GWR accepted approaches from the S&BR and S&CR, and these two companies were merged with the Paddington company in 1854. The outcome of this was that both the GWR and its bitter rival, the LNWR, had railway interests in Shropshire. Despite such intense rivalry, both companies went on to operate joint lines within the county, those between Wellington and Shrewsbury and between Shrewsbury and Hereford.

Other main line companies were present in Shropshire, including the North Staffordshire Railway (NSR), whose line from Stoke-on-Trent to Market Drayton was of little importance, being busy only on market days. After the 'grouping' of 1923, the NSR, like the LNWR, became part of the London Midland and Scottish Railway. A more important company which ran through Shropshire was the Cambrian Railways system, whose headquarters were in Oswestry, its main line running from Shrewsbury to Aberystwyth in mid-Wales and Pwllheli in north Wales. The Cambrian system was absorbed by the GWR in 1922, just before the 'grouping'. There were other standard gauge lines in the county: the Montgomery and Shropshire Railway, one of Colonel Stephens' empire of impecunious little railways, and the Bishop's Castle Railway.

The GWR was destined to become the most important railway company in Shropshire, its Paddington–Birkenhead expresses running through the county, between Wolverhampton and Chester, via Shrewsbury. After its absorption of the Cambrian Railways, the company also operated the famous 'Cambrian Coast Express' between Paddington and Aberystwyth/Pwllheli, locomotives being changed at Shrewsbury. Famous GWR express locomotives, like 'Star', 'Castle', 'Hall', 'County', and, later, 'King' class 4–6–0s were a familiar sight at the head of expresses between Wolverhampton, Shrewsbury and Chester. The Paddington company also had several local branches, one of the most important being the Severn Valley Railway, which ran from Shrewsbury to Hartlebury, near Droitwich, Worcestershire, and passed through such places as Coalport, Ironbridge and Buildwas. A section of this line, between Bridgnorth and Kidderminster, has become famous as a preserved railway operating superbly restored steam locomotives, coaches and wagons. The section between Bridgnorth and Highley lies within Shropshire, and these stations, along with the rest on the SVR, have been beautifully restored.

The LNWR also had an important line between Shrewsbury and Crewe, where famous express locomotives which had been repaired at Crewe could often be seen 'running in' at the head of local trains. The company had a few branch lines, but these were not as numerous as those of the GWR.

The railway network in Shropshire remained virtually intact until the advent of Dr Beeching's infamous 'Reshaping Report', which advocated total closure of branch lines all over Great Britain. The county was not immune from this rationalization, and all of the branches in the county were closed in the 1960s. Nowadays, all that remains of a once complex system is the old GWR line between Chester and Wolverhampton, which carries only local traffic, express trains now running via Crewe and Stafford, and the old joint line between Shrewsbury and Hereford, along with the ex-LNWR line between Crewe and Shrewsbury. Trains between Crewe and Cardiff use this line. The only other route still open is the ex-Cambrian Railways line between Shrewsbury and Aberystwyth/Pwllheli. However, it is still possible to enjoy the great days of the steam railway in Shropshire, thanks to the efforts of everyone at the Severn Valley Railway. There are also main line steam excursions between Chester and Hereford, via Shrewsbury.

In preparing this book on the railways in Shropshire, we hope that we have conveyed memories of the once complex system that existed in the county before Dr Beeching did his worst, and of the many local stations that were once part of the landscape and lifeblood of the area in the days before private cars and heavy lorries. Above all, we hope that much enjoyment is derived from the book. We certainly had a great deal of pleasure in putting the whole project together.

The quality of some of the photographs included in this book is not ideal, but we felt that they were worth including because some show rare events or locations not often seen in photographic form. Others have been used to complete a necessary part of the story of particular locations. We sincerely hope that the use of these pictures does not detract too much from readers' enjoyment.

Postcard of a local manufacturer's site at Craven Arms. In view is the station and the main Shrewsbury–Hereford joint line.

THE GWR MAIN LINE

Ex-GWR 'Castle' class 4–6–0 no. 5088 Llanthony Abbey *at the head of a Birkenhead–Paddington express at Admaston on the Shrewsbury and Birmingham Railway section of the GWR main line between Wolverhampton and Shrewsbury. The locomotive was built in February 1939, its name taken from 'Star' class locomotive no. 4068, which had been withdrawn in November 1938. Admaston Halt closed altogether on 7 September 1964.*

The first station out of Wolverhampton and in Shropshire is at Albrighton, pictured here in the 1950s. The main building is shown, along with the ornate GWR footbridge, a feature of many of that company's wayside stations. The S&BR opened between Oakengates and Wolverhampton on 12 November 1849 and immediately ran into trouble with the mighty LNWR when it wished to load goods from its line on to narrow boats at Victoria Basin canal wharf, Wolverhampton. A battle arose here because the LNWR jointly owned the last half mile of line into the town, alongside the Birmingham canal basin, where transshipment could take place, and were keen to prevent the S&BR having access to the canal. What became known as the 'Riot at Temporary Station' involved several hundred navvies fighting each other, and police and soldiers were involved in breaking up this orchestrated battle. Such was the bad feeling between the two companies, that the S&BR sought friendly relations with the GWR.

The road entrance to Albrighton station, 1950s. The S&BR amalgamated with the GWR on 1 September 1854, after the LNWR had made several, often illegal, attempts to take over the little Shrewsbury company without success. From November of that year, S&BR trains ran through to Wolverhampton's Low Level station instead of the LNWR High Level one as had been originally planned. Albrighton station was provided with goods facilities which were closed on 7 September 1964.

Another view of the drive to Albrighton station as it appeared in the 1930s.

An unidentified ex-GWR 'Modified Hall' class 4–6–0 with straight-sided Hawkesworth tender on a Birkenhead–Paddington express approaching Shifnal station, mid-1950s. The S&BR never actually reached Birmingham over its own metals, having a share in the LNWR Stour Valley line. With the GWR approaching Wolverhampton, where it would link up with the S&BR, the LNWR refused to open its Stour Valley route, which had been completed in the 1850s. The S&BR, although now part of the GWR, announced that it was to start operating through trains to Birmingham from 1 December 1852. In a well-publicized attempt to reach New Street, the S&BR despatched a train from Wolverhampton High Level station only to come buffer-to-buffer with LNWR locomotive *Swift*. The local populace were at the lineside to witness another potential riot, but the only outcome was that writs were served. In the event, the S&BR obtained access to Birmingham from 4 February 1854, but its service was rather poor. Shifnal station remains open today, but goods traffic ceased from 7 January 1964.

Oakengates station, showing the station buildings and goods yard, complete with goods shed, 1950s. Goods facilities ceased from 4 January 1965, although the station remains open to passengers.

Oakengates, showing the tunnel at the Shrewsbury end. Difficulties in the construction of this tunnel allowed opening of the line between here and Wolverhampton only until 12 November 1850. From this date, the S&BR was opened throughout to Shrewsbury, where it met the Shrewsbury and Chester Railway, providing a through route between the West Midlands and the north-west of England at Chester, where both lines met the Birkenhead Railway for access to the lucrative Mersey seaports.

The station entrance and main building (on the extreme right of the picture) at Oakengates in the early years of the twentieth century.

The entrance to Wellington station, 1950s. In view are a proliferation of British Railways notices and timetables, the parcels office with BR parcels van outside, a motor car of the period, and a couple of female passengers leaving the station.

Wellington station platforms, 1950s. Wellington station was jointly owned by the LNWR/LMS, whose line joined the S&BR here, and the GWR. Wellington, always a prosperous town, became a junction of the two companies in 1849 with the opening of the S&BR and the Shropshire Union Railways and Canal Company line (SUR), owned by the LNWR. The SUR owned 29 miles of railway which comprised the Stafford-Wellington route and a half share in the line from Wellington to Shrewsbury. The remainder of the S&BR route to Shrewsbury was always jointly owned by the GWR and LNWR. The LNWR used these two lines in its attempts to prevent the GWR reaching the Mersey and tapping lucrative traffic emanating from there. In order to bring the GWR to heel, the LNWR began a price war, which brought ridiculously low fares between Wolverhampton and Shrewsbury. The S&BR line between Wolverhampton and Shrewsbury was some 26 miles long, while the LNWR route was over 40 miles, running as it did along the main line between Wolverhampton and Stafford, then along the SUR to Wellington and finally the joint line to Shrewsbury. Between 1849 and 1853, fares were 1s first class, 9d second class, and 6d third class. As a comparison, fares between Wellington and Shrewsbury over the joint line were 6d, 3d, and 1d for the 10¼ miles. The LNWR was losing a considerable amount of money pursuing this policy, but the Euston company could afford to stand the loss if it succeeded in forcing the GWR out of Merseyside. In the event the ploy failed and both companies competed for Mersey traffic over many years.

In this view, trains of both the GWR and LMS are present. On the left is a 2–6–2 tank locomotive of the LMS at the head of a train for Shrewsbury, while a GWR 2–6–2 'Prairie Tank' waits at the platform on the right. The GWR also had a locoshed here (BR code 84H) which provided locomotives for traffic over the branch between Wellington and Crewe, via Market Drayton, as well as supplying engines for freight traffic in the area. It also had a sub-shed at Much Wenlock. The shed's allocation usually consisted of 0–6–0 and 2–6–2 tank locomotives as well as 2–6–0 freight locomotives. Trains operating over the LMS route had locomotives supplied by Stafford shed.

Wellington station as viewed from the island platform, 1950s.

The station throat at Wellington in the 1950s, showing Wellington no. 3 signalbox and a BR upper quadrant home starting signal. The station remains open, serving the overspill town of Telford, and has been renamed Wellington Telford West.

Wellington Joint station at the turn of the century, with a GWR local train at the platform. This atmospheric view shows much of the early twentieth-century station, including a W.H. Smith's bookstall, a common sight on many of Britain's railway stations at this time. Also in view is a passenger, complete with straw boater, and station staff. There are milk churns next to a station roof support, and ornate station lamps.

Ex-LMS 4F 0–6–0 no. 44435 heads a mixed goods train, possibly for Stafford, through Walcot station on the joint line, 1950s. Walcot station closed altogether on 7 September 1964.

Ex-GWR 2–8–0 locomotive no. 3825 heads a mixed freight train through Upton Magna station, on the joint line, on its way to Wolverhampton. This neat little station was closed to passengers on 7 September 1963 and to goods on 4 May 1964.

The handsome exterior of Shrewsbury station during the Edwardian period. The station drive is filled with hansom cabs, the taxis of the time.

The main platform at Shrewsbury station, with the main building behind. The platform is littered with barrows loaded with parcels.

Another view of the platforms at Shrewsbury, again littered with barrows, one of which is loaded with mailbags. In the background is a Western Region 'Warship' class diesel-hydraulic locomotive at the head of a Paddington–Birkenhead express.

Shrewsbury's Abbey Foregate station just after the 'Grouping' of 1923. A local train made up of rather ramshackle coaches has just arrived. The locomotive of LNWR origin and numbered 8108 stands at the water tower to await filling of its tender tank.

The terminus of Colonel Stephens' Shropshire and Montgomery Railway (S&MR) was at Shrewsbury West station, seen here with locomotive no. 3 of uncertain parentage attached to a guard's van. The little 0–6–0 is being attended to by her driver. The S&MR was originally planned to run from mid-Wales to Stoke-on-Trent, but never reached any further than Shrewsbury, but it did obtain the nickname of 'The Pots' because of its intended destination in The Potteries. Shrewsbury West station closed to passengers on 6 November 1933, but was retained for use as a parcels depot until 29 February 1960, when it closed altogether.

Ex-GWR 'Dean Goods' 0–6–0 no. 2516 awaits departure from the bay platform at Shrewsbury station at 2.05 p.m. with a local service, probably along the ex-Cambrian Railways section, as these 'Dean Goods' locomotives were usually allocated to ex-Cambrian sheds during the 1950s, when this picture was taken. Shrewsbury developed as a major railway crossroads from around 1848, when the Shrewsbury and Chester Railway built a temporary terminus here. The Shrewsbury and Birmingham and Shropshire Union (later LNWR) Railways arrived in 1849 and a shared station arose. Soon afterwards, the Shrewsbury and Hereford Railway arrived. After various arguments, the joint Shrewsbury station arose, which was under the control of the GWR and LNWR (later the LMS) by 1862. It was situated high above the town and originally occupied the area on the north bank of the Severn, later to occupy the south bank as well. The station was covered by an overall roof which was removed at the north end just after the 'Grouping', at a time when trains from the Cambrian Railways system, which had been absorbed by the GWR in 1922, also used the joint station. The remainder of the roof was removed in 1963. The old S&BR station at Abbey Foregate was closed to passengers on 30 September 1912 and to goods on 1 August 1963. The old S&CR station closed on 1 June 1849. Other closures at Shrewsbury included Abbey station (NSR), which closed to passengers on 6 November 1933 and to goods on 7 October 1968; Coleham goods yard of the Shrewsbury and Hereford Joint Railway, which closed on 15 August 1966; English Bridge (GWR/LNWR), which closed on 2 May 1898; Greenfield Siding (GWR), which closed on 6 May 1968; SU Yard (LNWR), which closed on 5 April 1971.

In steam days, the LNWR and LMS put engines which had been newly built at Crewe, or which had been under heavy repair, on running-in turns, hauling three-coach local trains between Crewe and Shrewsbury in the morning and on stopping trains from Crewe to Manchester (London Road) in the afternoon. These local trains could be hauled by top-link locomotives, including 'Princess-Royal' and 'Princess-Coronation' Pacifics. In this case, it was newly built BR Standard class 8P Pacific no. 71000 *Duke of Gloucester* on its first revenue-earning trip after being built in May 1954. In this view, the locomotive had brought its train into Shrewsbury and is seen at the 180 lever Severn Bridge signal-box. The usual departure time for this train for Crewe was about noon.

The same locomotive is running light into Shrewsbury station after turning ready to return to Crewe. This locomotive was a three-cylinder, Caprotti valve-geared Pacific and was destined to be the only one to be built by BR, although there were probably plans to build more. Unfortunately, the locomotive did not steam very well and was not a great success. Because of the experimental nature of the engine, it was always shedded at Crewe and was generally used on express services between London, Birmingham and the north-west of England. When the west coast main line was modernized in the early 1960s, and electric traction introduced for expresses between Crewe and London, no. 71000 became surplus to requirements and was withdrawn late in 1962. She eventually went to Woodham Brothers, Barry, South Wales, and was left to rot there until preservationists took her to the Great Central Railway in April 1974. Work on full restoration was undertaken, and this was completed by May 1986. She returned to main line duties, hauling enthusiasts' specials, in 1989. The restorers fitted a Kylchap blastpipe (as originally suggested by her designers) and new ashpan, which improved her performance greatly. She can be seen frequently on enthusiasts' specials, often running from her 'birthplace' to Holyhead.

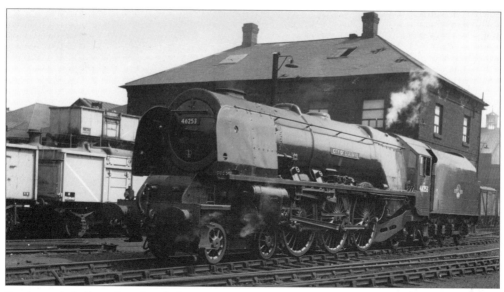

Standing outside Shrewsbury locoshed is ex-LMS 'Princess-Coronation' Pacific no. 46253, *City of St Albans*. The engine has probably been under heavy repair at Crewe and has just completed a running-in turn. Shrewsbury shed was opened in 1856 by the Shrewsbury and Hereford Railway and became jointly owned by the GWR and LNWR. In GWR days the shed was coded SaLoP and it became 84G when first nationalized. It was renumbered 89A in January 1961 and 6D in September 1963. The shed finally closed on 6 November 1967. Its LMS allocation included Stanier 'Black Five' 4–6–0s and 'Jubilee' class 4–6–0s. There were also allocations of LMS 3F 0–6–0s, 2–6–2, 2–6–4, and 3F tank locomotives. Freight locomotives included 8F 2–8–0s and ex-LNWR 0–8–0s. As late as 1945, two ex-LNWR Webb 2–4–2 tanks were shedded there. The GWR allocation on 31 December 1947, the day before nationalization, was as follows:

GWR 'Wolverhampton' 0–6–0PT	2745
GWR Collett 0–6–0PT	3602, 3615, 3702, 3782, 3788, 4602, 4623, 4672, 5774, 9657, 9719
GWR Collett 0–6–2T	5642, 5673, 6606, 6633
GWR Churchward 2–6–2T	4118, 5154, 5168
GWR Collett 0–6–0	2228, 2229, 2231, 2233, 2234, 2235, 3217
GWR Churchward 2–6–0	6307, 6338, 6348
GWR Churchward 2–8–0	2897
GWR Dean 'Bulldog' 4–4–0	3377
	3442 *Bullfinch*
GWR Collett 'Dukedog' 4–4–0	9024, 9073, 9076
GWR Collett 'Hall' class 4–6–0	4919 *Donnington Hall*
	5981 *Frensham Hall*
	5994 *Roydon Hall*
GWR Hawksworth 'Modified Hall' class 4–6–0	6963 *Throwley Hall*
	6976 *Graythwaite Hall*
	6980 *Llanrumney Hall*
GWR Churchward 'Star' class 4–6–0	4040 *Queen Boadicea*
	4044 *Prince George*
	4046 *Princess Mary*
	4061 *Glastonbury Abbey*
GWR Collett 'Castle' class 4–6–0	5021 *Whittington Castle*
	5032 *Usk Castle*
	5061 *Earl of Birkenhead*
	5064 *Bishop's Castle*
	5073 *Blenheim*
	5086 *Viscount Horne*
	5097 *Sarum Castle*
	7006 *Lydford Castle*

TOTAL 53

On leaving Shrewsbury in the direction of Chester, the GWR main line traverses the Shrewsbury and Chester Railway (S&CR), its first station being Leaton, pictured here in the 1930s. Like the S&BR, the S&CR came into conflict with the LNWR because of arrangements it made, along with the S&BR, for interchange of goods traffic with the Birkenhead Railway at Chester. The S&BR and S&CR came to an agreement to carry freight from the Mersey, via the Birkenhead Railway, to the industrial West Midlands, thereby threatening LNWR monopoly in the north-west. Leaton station closed to passengers on 12 September 1960 and to goods on 15 March 1965.

The exterior of Baschurch station, a rather handsome structure. In an effort to bring the S&CR into line, the LNWR threatened the company at Chester by issuing written threats. When this did not work a ban was put on the issue of through tickets from Chester to Birmingham, via Shrewsbury, and the poor S&CR ticket clerk was physically ejected from Chester station. In an attempt to starve the Shrewsbury companies of freight traffic, the Birkenhead Railway (a satellite of the LNWR) was forced to boycott as much S&CR traffic as it legally could. In the end, like the S&BR, the S&CR sought alliance with the GWR, which brought about the competition that the LNWR had tried to avoid when the S&CR amalgamated with the Paddington company at the same time as the S&BR.

Baschurch station, showing the substantial main station building. The station closed to passengers on 12 September 1960 and to goods on 5 July 1965.

Rednal and West Felton station as it appeared at the turn of the century, showing its main building, signal-box and goods siding well filled with freight wagons. Also in view are the station staff. The station closed to passengers on 12 September 1960 and to goods on 7 October 1963.

Whittington Low Level station, 1950s. The station was an interchange with the Cambrian Railways line between Whitchurch and Oswestry, this company having its own High Level station situated behind the one pictured here.

Another view of the S&CR Whittington Low Level station, 1950s. This station closed to passengers on 12 September 1960 and to goods on 7 October 1963. The Cambrian Railways High Level station closed on 4 January 1960.

The fine Italianate main building at Gobowen station near the dawn of the age of the motor car. A Model T Ford, the first mass-produced car, stands just in front of the building. It was this mass-production that was to eventually lead to the growth of private car ownership, particularly after the Second World War, and bring about the almost complete demise of the railways. With roads so choked with motor vehicles, the railways could yet make a comeback, but much depends on the outcome of railway privatization.

Another exterior view of Gobowen station, a little later than the previous one. The station remains open today to serve local traffic, the old GWR main line being now only a secondary route between Chester and Wolverhampton, via Shrewsbury. Today, there are no glamorous express trains, just DMU 'Sprinter' trains calling at all stations that remain open. The line has often been threatened with closure but it survives as an important commuter route.

The interior of Gobowen station, complete with station staff and steam railmotor train, operating a local service between Chester and Shrewsbury. Goods traffic ceased operating out of Gobowen from 2 November 1964.

Exterior of Preesgweene station, with station staff standing at the level-crossing. The station was renamed Weston Rhyn in February 1935 and lies between Gobowen and Chirk. Closure to passengers was on 12 September 1960 and to goods on 4 November 1963. From here, the line goes on through Chirk and into Flintshire before entering Chester.

SECTION TWO

GWR BRANCHES

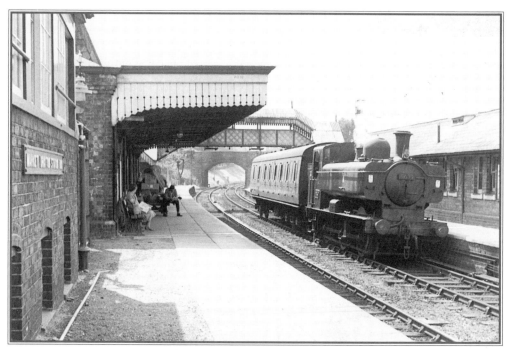

Ex-GWR 0–6–0 pannier tank no. 9677 waits at Market Drayton station with a one-coach local train to Wellington. The station was situated on the Wellington–Nantwich branch.

Adderley station, on the Nantwich–Market Drayton section of the branch between Nantwich and Wellington. This branch gave the GWR access to the LNWR heartland at Crewe, the company having its own platform and staff there. The line was built by the Nantwich and Market Drayton Railway, being absorbed by the GWR in 1897. The very attractive setting and rural nature of the station can be clearly seen. The signalman and a solitary passenger (complete with straw boater) pose for the camera.

Adderley station on a wet day in the 1950s. The station had its own small goods yard, just behind the signal-box, which lasted until 3 February 1964, the passenger station having closed on 9 September 1963.

RAILWAY STATION & CATTLE MARKET, MARKET DRAYTON.
PERFECTION SERIES 1362.

A turn-of-the-century view of Market Drayton station. Market Drayton has been an important market town since being granted its charter by Henry III on 8 November 1245, and the town was, naturally, an important goal for the railway companies. Three railway companies entered the town, making Market Drayton station a major junction. The North Staffordshire Railway had its only route into Shropshire, as the Silverdale and Market Drayton Railway, which was authorized in 1864 and opened in 1870. It was built to prevent the GWR having an independent route to Manchester via Northwich. The second company was the previously mentioned Nantwich and Market Drayton Railway (N&MDR), which made a head-on connection with the GWR's 16¼ mile line, the Wellington and Drayton Railway, which had been incorporated in 1862 to link the N&MDR with the main GWR network. The Wellington–Nantwich line was classed as a secondary route and had little local value to the GWR, as passenger trains were very few and stations were far apart. They were little-used and the line was under threat well before Beeching took an interest, but it managed to survive until 1963.

Despite having little value as a passenger route, Market Drayton's importance brought much freight traffic to its sidings, as can be seen in this 1950s view. An ex-GWR 2–6–0 locomotive departs from the station with another freight train on what appears to be market day. The station did have a passenger role in the years up to and after the First World War, as young girls left here, and many similar stations, to go into service. One girl to leave from Market Drayton station to enter service was Rose Williams. She first went from her home town to Liverpool, thence to Birmingham and, finally, to Clayton Hall in Staffordshire. From there, she went to Penmaenmawr in north Wales, where she married. She returned home very infrequently over the next fifty years.

Market Drayton station, looking towards Wellington, 1950s. Plenty of freight vans are occupying the sidings here. Today, very little of the old station remains.

A GWR advertisement for Sunday excursions to Wolverhampton and Birmingham, December 1933. Even if such a journey were possible today, the fare to Birmingham would be substantially more than 5s.

An unidentified ex-LMS Ivatt 2–6–2 tank locomotive waits at Market Drayton station not long before its closure at the head of a Stephenson's Locomotive Society special.

BR 'Austerity' 2–8–0 locomotive no. 90485 waits at Market Drayton to collect a freight train while an Ivatt 2–6–2 tank arrives with a local train from Crewe to Wellington, early 1963. A young train-spotter watches proceedings at the station.

MARKET DRAYTON. G.W.R.

A view of Market Drayton station in GWR days, looking towards Nantwich. Once again, several goods wagons occupy the sidings and goods shed on the far right. Like the rest of the branch, the station closed to passengers on 9 September 1963. Goods facilities, however, remained important to British Railways and the yards remained open until 1 May 1967, some two years after such facilities closed elsewhere along this particular line.

An unidentified ex-GWR 0–6–0 pannier tank runs through Tern Hill station with a 'pick-up' goods train. Tern Hill is still well known as a Royal Air Force base. In the years before the First World War, Rose Williams (see p. 32), as a young girl, would walk through the country lanes between Market Drayton and Tern Hill with six or seven friends, and catch the train from Tern Hill station back to Market Drayton. She thought then that the train ride was 'wonderful', the fare no more than a few pence. Tern Hill station closed to passengers on 9 September 1963 and to goods on 10 August 1964.

An unidentified ex-LMS Ivatt 2–6–2 tank locomotive pauses at Hodnet station with a two-coach local train from Crewe to Wellington.

Ex-GWR 0–6–0 pannier tank no. 9639 enters Hodnet station with a 'pick-up' goods train, 1950s.

The same locomotive waits at Hodnet signal-box before entering the station sidings to set down and pick up goods wagons before moving on to the next station along the line.

Railway Station, Hodnet

Hodnet station, looking towards Nantwich, 1930s. Its GWR origins are clear in its main building architecture. Such was the poor nature of the passenger service on the branch that on market days the North Staffordshire Railway was allowed to operate its passenger trains along the branch from Market Drayton to Hodnet. Although most passenger services were operated by 0–6–0 or 2–6–2 tank locomotives, sometimes, as the end of steam traction drew ever nearer, local trains could be seen in the hands of 4–6–0 locomotives of the 'Hall' class as they became redundant on express services, their role having been usurped by Western Region diesel-hydraulic locomotives. The station at Hodnet closed to passengers on 9 September 1963, and to goods on 10 August 1964. Today, no trace of the station buildings or platforms remains, but the old goods shed is still in existence, in use as part of a coal yard.

A turn-of-the-century view of Crudgington station, with station staff and a woman passenger with her daughter, both of whom are dressed in the fashion of the period.

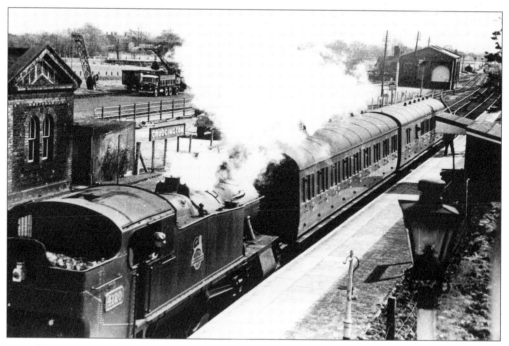

Some fifty years later at Crudgington station, with ex-GWR 2–6–2 Prairie tank no. 4120 waiting at the station with a local train. The station closed to passengers on 9 September 1963 and to goods on 3 May 1965.

Neen Sollars station on the Woofferton branch, which left the Severn Valley line at Bewdley, Worcestershire, ran through the Wyre Forest and joined the Shrewsbury–Hereford joint line south of Ludlow. The Woofferton branch was usually operated by GWR 0–6–0 pannier tanks throughout its life. Neen Sollars station, along with the rest of the branch, closed to passengers on 1 August 1962. Freight facilities at Neen Sollars survived a little longer, closure not coming until 6 January 1964.

KIDDERMINSTER, BEWDLEY, TENBURY WELLS, and WOOFFERTON

Miles	Up		a.m 🅰		a.m a.m		a.m X		p.m p.m X 🅰		p.m p.m p.m K N X			
	Kidderminster ¶......dep		..	..	.. 8 50	..	1018	..	2 10 ..	..	4 38 4 38 6 25	..	..	
3½	Bewdley 136. 139....{ arr / dep		..	..	8 59 / 9 0	..	1027 / 1029	..	2 19 .. / 2 25 ..	..	4 47 4 47 6 35 / 4 49 4 49 6 36	..	..	
8	Wyre Forest		..	..	9 11	..	1040	..	2 36 ..	..	5 0 5 0 6 47	..	..	
10	Cleobury Mortimer........		..	..	9 18	..	1047	..	2 44 ..	..	5 8 5 8 6 53	..	..	
13½	Neen Sollars.............		..	..	9 25	..	1055	..	2 51 ..	..	5 15 5 15 7 0	..	..	
15½	Newnham Bridge...........		..	..	9 30	..	11 1	..	2 56 ..	..	5 20 5 20 7 6	..	..	
19	Tenbury Wells......{ arr / dep	7 58	..	9 36 / 8 45 9 40	..	11 7 / 11 9	..	3 2 .. / 3 10 4 46	..	5 26 5 26 7 12 / 5 28 5 40 7 14	..	..	
21½	Easton Court ₭............	8 3	..	8 50 9 45	..	1114	..	3 15 4 51	..	5 33 5 45 7 19	..	..	
24½	Woofferton 488, 489.. arr	8 8	..	8 55 9 50	..	1119	..	3 20 4 56	..	5 38 5 50 7 24	..	..	

Miles	Down		a.m 🅰		a.m a.m X 🅰		a.m a.m X		p.m p.m X 🅰		p.m p.m			
	Woofferton .... dep	7 40	..	8 9 8 30	..	10 5 1150	..	3 47 4 33	..	5 55 7 55	..	..	
2½	Easton Court ₭...........	7 46	..	8 15 8 36	..	1011 1156	..	3 53 4 39	..	6 1 8 1	..	..	
5½	Tenbury Wells......{ arr / dep	7 50	..	8 19 8 40 / 8 20 ..	..	1015 12 0 / 1020 1213	..	3 57 4 43 / 4 0 ..	..	6 5 8 5 / .. 8 7	..	..	
8½	Newnham Bridge...........	..	..	8 28 ..	..	1028 1222	..	4 8 ..	..	.. 8 15	..	..	
10½	Neen Sollars.............	..	..	8 34 ..	..	1034 1228	..	4 14 ..	..	.. 8 21	..	..	
14½	Cleobury Mortimer........	..	..	8 44 ..	..	1048 1240	..	4 23 ..	..	.. 8 31	..	..	
16½	Wyre Forest...........	..	..	8 49 ..	..	1053 1246	..	4 28 ..	..	.. 8 36	..	..	
20½	Bewdley ¶ 136, 139..{ arr / dep	..	..	8 57 / 9 0 ..	..	11 1 1255 / 11 3 1 2	..	4 36 .. / 4 48 ..	..	.. 8 44 / .. 8 46	..	..	
24½	Kidderminster 118 .... arr	..	..	9 10 ..	..	1112 1 11	..	4 57 ..	..	.. 8 55	..	..	

𝕂 Sta. for Little Hereford (¼ mile).
K Fris. and Sats.
N Except Fris. and Sats.
X Third class only. Limited accommodation
🅰 Thirdclass only.

¶ "Halt" at Foley Park between Kidderminster and Bewdley.

LOCAL TRAINS between Kidderminster and Bewdley, see page 138

A GWR timetable for the Woofferton branch, January 1947.

THE SEVERN VALLEY RAILWAY

Bridgnorth station at the turn of the century, with what looks like a GWR 4–4–0 locomotive at the head of a local train for Hartlebury, near Droitwich, Worcestershire. Bridgnorth is famous today as the starting point of the beautifully preserved Severn Valley Railway (SVR) to Kidderminster.

The Severn Valley Railway linked Shrewsbury with Hartlebury, near Droitwich, and was opened in 1862, construction beginning in 1858. The line was absorbed by the GWR in the 1870s. Its 40 mile route was single track all the way. The line was never a financial success, although it was well used by Birmingham anglers on summer Sundays, and it was closed to through-passenger traffic in 1963. Track between Shrewsbury and Bridgnorth was lifted to make way for the Telford bypass. Freight traffic continued south of Alveley Colliery until 1970, when the line was finally closed. The first station out from Shrewsbury was at Berrington, seen here shortly before closure with a local train at the platform. Since closure, the main station building, on the left of the picture, has become a private house.

After leaving Berrington, the line passed through Cound Halt and then entered Cressage station, seen here from the level-crossing and showing the main station building, which, like Berrington, has become a private house since closure on 9 September 1963. Also in view are the signal-box and goods siding.

Buildwas station with a local train entering, hauled by an unidentified ex-LMS 2–6–2 tank locomotive. Buildwas, some 12¼ miles from Shrewsbury, was the most important junction on the SVR. It was also the railhead for the original Ironbridge power station, which had been built in 1932 and had extensive sidings to serve it. Buildwas Junction opened with the rest of the SVR in 1862 and was a two-level junction station, the lower level being for the SVR, while the upper level was for the Craven Arms–Wellington line.

Another view of Buildwas station, with the power station on the left. A new power station was built on the western side of the junction station, and opened in 1970. The new power station has mechanized facilities for 'Merry Go Round' trains from Madeley Junction. The old power station was decommissioned when the new one opened.

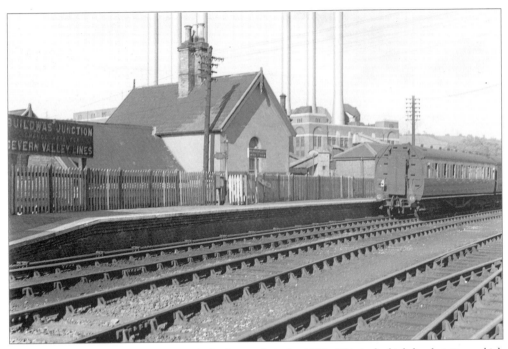

Buildwas station, with power station in the background, in the 1950s. This is the high-level station, which served the Craven Arms to Wellington line.

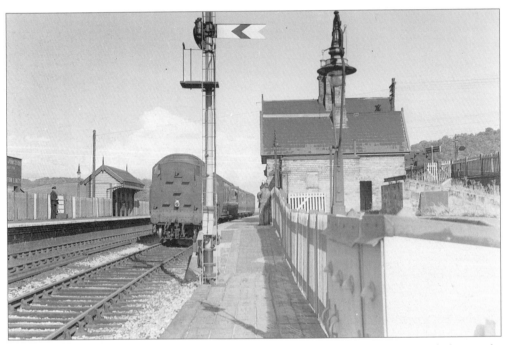

Buildwas low-level station, which served the SVR, with a rake of suburban coaches at the platform in the 1950s. Since closure in 1963, nothing of the station and its sidings remains. Most of the old station is now part of a golf course.

The line from Wellington to Much Wenlock and Craven Arms was opened in the 1860s and closed to passengers in 1962. Here the station of Horsehay and Dawley is seen as it was before the First World War. The single platform had a neat little station building and a smart wooden signal-cabin at the platform end.

Horseyhay and Dawley station on 11 September 1907, with local children posing on the platform. Note the advertisement for 'Nectar Tea'. Whatever happened to the enamel sign, or the brand name?

A busy scene at Horsehay and Dawley station at the turn of the century. Passengers dressed in the fashion of the day await the local service, which is approaching. Horsehay and Dawley station was the fifth station on the line from Wellington; the others were Ketley, Ketley Town Halt, New Dale Halt and Lawley Bank. All were closed to passengers on 23 July 1962. Horsehay and Dawley and Ketley had goods sidings, both of which closed on 6 July 1964. Since closure, a section of railway was taken over by the Telford Horsehay Steam Trust, who operate a selection of small tank locomotives and rolling stock over a short section of line. In 1982 the trust owned locomotives and rolling stock as listed below:

GWR 5600 class 0–6–2T   5619 (built 1925)

Industrial locomotives
Andrew Barclay (782) 0–6–0ST   *Peter* (built 1896)
North British (27414) 0–4–0D   *Tom* (built 1954)
Sentinel (9535) 4wVBT   (built 1952)
Ruston Hornsby (382824) 4wDM   VL6 (built 1955)

Rolling stock
1 ex-GWR auto-trailer
1 Wickham Trolley
Various wagons

In that year, the trust was open to visitors on Tuesday and Thursday evening, all day Saturday, and Sunday morning. Its one disadvantage is that it has to compete with the very much larger Severn Valley Railway, but a trip to this area could combine a visit to both railways, which are very different in character.

From Horsehay and Dawley, the line from Wellington passed through Doseley Halt, Lightmoor Platform and Greenbank Halt before reaching Coalbrookdale. Coalbrookdale will forever have its place in history as the village where the Industrial Revolution began when Abraham Darby began smelting iron using coke instead of charcoal in 1709, and casting molten iron in sand. Ironworks proliferated in the area at that time, and it is no surprise that it was served by the railways from 1862. Here, Coalbrookdale station is seen at the turn of the century. Its main building, on the left, and wooden waiting shelter, on the right, are typical of GWR wayside station architecture and appear to be very well kept. The station was provided with goods sidings, although the location appears to be very rural, given that it was once such an important ironworks centre. Incidentally, the iron Victoria Bridge over which the Severn Valley Railway crosses the river Severn near Arley was manufactured at Coalbrookdale and is a handsome example of iron engineering of the mid-nineteenth century.

Coalbrookdale station at the end of the 1950s. Coalbrookdale was also the junction of the Madeley branch, which became important as an access route for 'Merry Go Round' trains to the new Ironbridge power station. The line was important to the GWR because it provided profitable traffic from the ironworks in the area.

Another 1950s view of Coalbrookdale station. It closed to passengers on 23 July 1962, and to goods on 6 July 1964. A section of line from Ketley to Horsehay was retained to serve the ironworks at Horsehay, but this closed in 1981.

After leaving Coalbrookdale, the line passed through Buildwas Junction and then entered Farley Halt, with its primitive waiting shelter, mid-1950s.

Another view of Farley Halt in the 1950s, looking rather dilapidated. The little halt closed to passengers on 23 July 1962.

From Farley Halt, the line continued to Much Wenlock, seen here at the turn of the century.

Much Wenlock station as it appeared some fifty years later, with a local train waiting at the single platform.

Another turn-of-the-century view of Much Wenlock station, its handsome main station building covered in ivy, which gives it a very rural appearance. This is the second station to serve the town; the first closed on 1 August 1884 after this one had opened. Although the station had only one platform, and trains could not be crossed here, Much Wenlock was provided with extensive goods facilities, including a goods yard and shed. There was also a single road locoshed, a sub-shed of Wellington. In 1951, passenger services between Craven Arms and Much Wenlock ceased, which meant that the locoshed was surplus to requirements and it closed at the same time. Passenger services between Much Wenlock and Craven Arms carried on until 1962, so the station still had an important role for another decade. Much Wenlock station closed to passengers on 23 July 1962, but it survived for goods use until 2 December 1963.

After leaving Much Wenlock, the line continued through Westwood Halt, Presthope and Easthope Halt before reaching Longville, seen here with a DMU special train at the platform after it had closed for regular passenger use. All of the above stations closed to passengers on 31 December 1951. Longville and Presthope also had goods facilities, which were taken out of use on 2 December 1963.

The next station from Longville was Rushbury, seen here 26 October 1905. The main station building was similar to others on the route. The station closed altogether on 31 December 1951. The final station on the branch was Harton Road, also closed at the end of 1951. From there, trains joined the Shrewsbury and Hereford joint line for the run to Craven Arms, where trains along the branch terminated.

Back on the Severn Valley line the next station after Buildwas was Ironbridge. The station was called 'Ironbridge and Broseley' and is seen here with the town rising up behind. It was a crossing point from the time it opened, and a train for Shrewsbury, hauled by a GWR 0–6–0 tender engine, waits at the platform, some time before the First World War. It appears that the main station building is having an extension added, the roof yet to be slated. Ironbridge was one of the towns involved in the Industrial Revolution, the first cast-iron bridge having been built there in 1777. This can be seen spanning the Severn here and remains preserved. The town is now the home of the Ironbridge Gorge Museum, which receives many thousands of visitors a year, though, sadly, none can come by rail as the station closed on 7 September 1963 and is now a car park.

After leaving Ironbridge and Broseley, the SVR ran through Jackfield Halt and then entered Coalport. The town was famous for the floral pottery produced there, and 'Coalport' still exists as a brand name, but Coalport china is now produced in Stoke-on-Trent. The station building at Coalport was a substantial affair, as were many on the SVR. The building survives as a private dwelling.

A GWR diesel railcar waits at Coalport station with a train for Shrewsbury. This station was situated on the western side of the Severn and the LNWR also had a station at Coalport, on the eastern bank of the river. The LNWR station was at the end of a branch from Hadley, near Wellington, which had been promoted with goods traffic in mind, although it served passengers until 1952. The LNWR Coalport station and branch closed in 1960, three years earlier than the GWR Coalport station.

On leaving Coalport, the SVR left the Severn gorge and industrial Shropshire. The next station on the line was Linley, a little over 18 miles from Shrewsbury. It was the most isolated station on the whole route, being built to serve the nearby Apley Estate. There was no public road access, and Apley Hall was connected to the station by a suspension bridge over the river. Linley was provided with a goods siding which closed in 1951 and from this time the station name changed from Linley to Linley Halt. The photograph here clearly dates from well before then, showing the station as 'Linley'. For such an isolated station its main building is very substantial. This building is now a private house.

Bridgnorth station viewed from Pampudding Hill, showing the very substantial station building and the goods yard behind the Shrewsbury-bound platform. This station opened in 1862 and is approached from the town by a long driveway. Access to the station from High Town was via a footbridge across the valley, seen here just beyond the signal-box. This bridge was closed in 1976. From Shrewsbury, the SVR approached Bridgnorth through a 550 yard tunnel which passed under High Town. This tunnel was built on a double curve which swung from the right and then the left.

Another view of Bridgnorth from above, with the footbridge to High Town clearly visible. The sidings in the foreground contain private owner wagons belonging to 'Eveson' and are full of coal. The siding behind the signal-box contains wagons belonging to Highley Colliery and to 'Wm Blake & Son' of Ludlow. There was little traffic on the roads around Bridgnorth, something that would change in the next few years.

Bridgnorth station, looking towards Kidderminster, 1950s. A local train for Bewdley and Droitwich waits at the platform, while passengers wait for a Shrewsbury-bound train. The sidings are full of closed vans, and other wagons can be seen beyond the passenger train. Various barrows litter the platform, one of which contains mailbags. Thanks to the efforts of the preservationists, the station looks little changed today.

Apart from the SVR, Bridgnorth is blessed with another railway. This is a cliff railway, which links High Town with Low Town. It is seen here in the early years of the twentieth century and continues to operate today. For a few pence, a ride on the cliff railway completes a day's visit to the preserved Severn Valley Railway.

On leaving Bridgnorth, the SVR crossed the five-arch Oldbury Viaduct – built to carry double tracks in connection with an abortive project to bring a line from Wolverhampton to Bridgnorth in the late nineteenth century – into Knowlesands Tunnel and then climbed at 1 in 100 to Eardington Summit and passed Eardington station. The line then descended at 1 in 100 for 1½ miles. After a further ¼ mile the line entered Hampton Loade station, its substantial main building pictured here before the First World War. The station was provided with a siding behind the waiting shelter on the right, this platform having been added in 1883. The location was always popular with anglers from Birmingham, and, in BR days, fishermen's trains often terminated here.

The next major station reached by the SVR from Hampton Loade was Highley, but just before Highley station, Alveley Halt once existed. This Halt served a nearby colliery, which closed in 1969. The Halt was not advertised in BR or GWR timetables and was used only to bring miners to the colliery. The colliery was situated on the other side of the river from the railway, and the railway siding serving the mine was connected by an aerial ropeway over a concrete bridge. The photograph shows Highley station in GWR days, complete with coal wagons from the local mine. In BR days the station had a footbridge but it had to be demolished by the SVR in 1974. From here, the SVR went on to Arley and into Worcestershire, heading towards Hartlebury.

Closure of the SVR by BR in 1963 should have spelt the end for the route, but, in 1965, a group of enthusiasts formed the Severn Valley Railway Society at Kidderminster. Their intention was to reopen a section of the line between Bridgnorth and Aveley and initial efforts raised 10 per cent of the £25,000 purchase price. Things could have turned out very differently, however, because, in July 1965, BR began to dismantle the railway system at Bridgnorth. Intervention by enthusiasts persuaded BR to stop demolition, thereby preserving the station for use by the private railway. Here, in the early years, one of the Severn Valley Railway steam locomotive acquisitions, ex-LMS Ivatt 2MT 2–6–0 no. 46443, lies in the old Bridgnorth station sidings. Note the little Austin A35 motor car, which helps to date the picture.

By 1967, the new SVR had acquired four passenger coaches and a locomotive, and the next three years were spent restoring the line and obtaining a Light Railway Order from the Department of the Environment. After some difficulty, an LRO was issued and the section from Bridgnorth to Hampton Loade, with an intermediate stop at Eardington, was opened to the public on 23 May 1970, and the remainder of the purchase price was paid shortly afterwards. A train from Hampton Loade, headed by ex-BR 4MT 2–6–4 tank locomotive no. 80079 built in Brighton in 1954, is seen here entering Bridgnorth station.

Ex-BR 4MT 2–6–4 tank locomotive no. 80079 takes on water in the sidings at Bridgnorth after bringing in its train. The locomotive retains its 33B, Tilbury, shed-plate. Bridgnorth station was not provided with a locoshed in GWR and BR days, so the SVR had to provide such facilities itself, not only to house the steam locomotives that it acquired, but also to provide covered accommodation for repairs and maintenance. Such facilities were built, and opened in 1977.

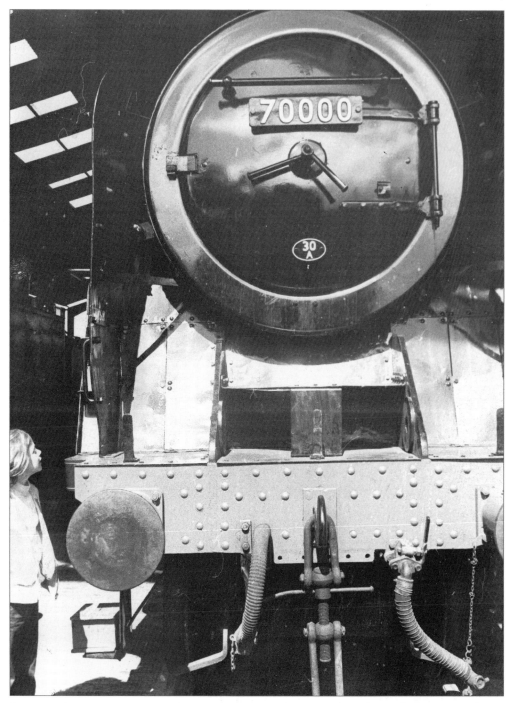

One steam locomotive acquisition that was not to remain long at Bridgnorth was the first BR Pacific no. 70000 *Britannia*, seen here inside the new locoshed and being admired by Marian Roberts. It carries the 30A shed-plate of Stratford, East London.

A view of the Bridgnorth locoshed from the station footbridge with some of the railway's locomotive collection in the yard. Included are ex-LMS Stanier 6P5F 2–6–0 no. 2968, ex-GWR 'Manor' class locomotive no. 7819 *Hinton Manor*, and ex-BR diesel-electric locomotive D7633, built in 1964. Just visible behind the locoshed is the new boiler shop built in the late 1980s.

Posed in the shed yard at Bridgnorth is ex-GWR 'Manor' class 4–6–0 no. 7802 *Bradley Manor*. Originally bought for spares to maintain the SVR's two other 'Manor' class locomotives, 7812 *Erlestoke Manor* and 7819 *Hinton Manor*, the locomotive has recently been fully restored at Bewdley.

A view of Bridgnorth station as it appears since preservation, with ex-GWR 2–6–0 no. 9303 in the shed yard. Unlike the main line years, when the SVR never made any money, the preserved SVR has been a great success, with turnover reaching some £2,736,438 in 1994.

The SVR does contract work for other locomotive owners, as well as maintaining its own fleet, which in 1994 brought in an income of £171,212. Here, ex-LNER A4 Pacific no. 60009 *Union of South Africa* stands in the shed yard after undergoing restoration for its owner.

Ex-GWR 0–6–0 pannier tank no. 7714, in BR black livery, waits to leave Bridgnorth with a train for Kidderminster. This 57XX class locomotive was built to a Collett design by Kerr Stewart & Co. of Stoke-on-Trent in 1930. Its works no. was 4449.

The attractive main station building at Bridgnorth, with signal-box in the background, as seen from the footbridge. The hanging flower-baskets enhance the overall appearance of the SVR Co. station. The SVR is set in a very attractive location, and is popular with film-makers, again bringing in revenue for the railway company. A new footbridge linking the station with High Town was built by the Bridgnorth Footbridge Trust and opened in 1994.

Ex-GWR 'Manor' class 4–6–0 no. 7819 *Hinton Manor* arrives at Hampton Loade station with a train from Bridgnorth to Bewdley. In this view she is painted in GWR livery, but is now in the BR black livery of the early 1950s. After Alveley Colliery was closed in 1969 and passenger services ceased at Bewdley in 1970, an appeal was mounted to raise £110,000, £74,000 of which was to purchase the railway from Alveley, through Bewdley, to Foley Park (near Kidderminster) to link with BR. With the support of local Conservative MP Sir Gerald Nabarro fund-raising was successful, and the efforts of the railway's volunteers allowed the line to open as far as Highley on 12 April 1974 and through to Bewdley on 18 May 1974. The line reached its final destination at Kidderminster on 30 July 1984.

The main station building at Hampton Loade from a Kidderminster-bound train.

The preserved goods yard and signal-box at Highley station with ex-Cadbury's goods vans in the siding. The railway owns several railway wagons which are dispersed over the whole route, adding a sense of a real railway. During enthusiasts' weekends, some of the SVR's collection of goods wagons are brought together to form period goods trains, which are popular with visitors.

The main station building at Highley station. Such has been the quality of the restoration of the stations on the SVR that Highley, along with Arley (the next station on the line for Bewdley), has won major awards in Best Restored Station competitions, as well as featuring in many film and television productions.

CAMBRIAN RAILWAYS

The exterior of Oswestry station, headquarters of the Cambrian Railways system.

Oswestry station, showing the substantial main building and platforms. The first railway to enter Oswestry was the Shrewsbury and Chester Railway branch from Gobowen, opened in 1848, with its intermediate station Park Hall Halt. It was, however, the Cambrian Railways which converted the quiet country town into a major industrial centre. Its first line, the Welshpool and Oswestry, arrived in 1860.

Cambrian Railways.

BIRMINGHAM CATTLE AND POULTRY SHOw, Bingley Hall;

National Dog Show, Curzon Hall;

NOVEMBER, 29th to 30th,

On Tuesday, Wednesday, and Thursday,

November 28th, 29th, and 30th,

Cheap 1 Day and 2 or 3 Days Tickets

Will be issued to

BIRMINGHAM

| | Times of Starting. | 3rd Class Return Fares |
| From | | |
Barmouth 7 52, Towyn 8 25, Aberdovey 8 85   1 Days Ticket 5s.   2 or 3 Days Ticket 9s.

Children under Three years of age, Free; above three and under Twelve years of age, Half-fare.

Holders of ONE DAY Tickets return from Birmingham (New Street) at 10 50 p.m. on date of issue of Ticket

Holders of Two or Three Days Ticket return from Birmingham (New Street) as under:—

Tickets issued on Nov. 28th will be available to return at 11 25 a.m. on Nov. 29th or 30th.

    „   „   Nov. 29th   „   „   „   Nov. 30th or Dec. 1st.

    „   „   Nov. 30th   „   „   „   Dec. 1st or 2nd.

All information regarding Excursion Trains and Tourist Arrangements on the Cambrian Railways may be had on application to Mr W. H. GOUGH, Superintendent of the Line, Oswestry.

Oswestry, Nov. 1899.

A Cambrian Railways advertisement for an exhibition in Birmingham, November 1899.

The platforms at Oswestry station in the 1950s. The first line proposed to reach Shropshire was the Llanidloes and Newtown Railway, incorporated in 1853, which immediately planned an extension to Oswestry and Shrewsbury. Engineers David Davies and Thomas Savin began work on the new route on 3 October 1855 and it opened for goods on 30 April 1859 and on 31 August for passengers. Meanwhile, another company had been formed for the Oswestry and Newtown section, which had received Royal Assent on 26 June 1855, and opened on 10 July 1861 with a service from Oswestry to Llanidloes.

Oswestry station between the wars, with a GWR saddle tank locomotive sandwiched between a pair of railmotor coaches at the far platform. After the line from Llanidloes opened, a new route, the Oswestry, Ellesmere and Whitchurch Railway, was authorized in 1861 and opened on 27 July 1864. In the same month these companies were merged to form Cambrian Railways and were joined by the Aberystwyth and Welsh Coast Railway in 1865. These lines became famous as the route of the 'Cambrian Coast Express'. Although really a Welsh company, the Cambrian established its headquarters at Oswestry and built its locoworks and carriage construction factory there in 1863.

The Cambrian was never a financial success, going bankrupt on more than one occasion, and it was absorbed by the GWR in 1922. This company could not make the system pay either, despite its popularity with summer tourists. Here, in BR days, ex-GWR 'Collett Goods' 0–6–0 stands at Oswestry station with a train for mid-Wales.

A local train headed by an unidentified GWR 0–6–0 pannier tank stands at the platform in Oswestry station. The Cambrian system was lightly laid and heavy locomotives could not use the route. It therefore became the preserve of GWR double-framed 'Duke of Cornwall' 4–4–0 locomotives and, from the 1930s, hybrid Collett 'Dukedog' 4–4–0s. These were replaced in the 1950s by 'Manor' class 4–6–0s which had been specially built for such lines and were a familiar sight on the 'Cambrian Coast Express'.

The Cambrian locoworks in GWR days, with Cambrian and GWR 0–6–0s in view. A locoshed also existed in Oswestry coded OSW in GWR days and 89A under BR ownership. The shed had some unusual engines in its allocation just before nationalization, as can be seen from this list compiled on 15 June 1947:

Alexandra Docks 0–6–0ST	680
Cambrian Railways 0–6–0	822, 823, 844, 849, 855, 873, 884, 887, 892, 893, 895, 896, 898
Cambrian Railways 2–4–0T	1196, 1197
Liskeard & Looe Railway 2–4–0T	1308 *Lady Margaret*
Whitland & Cardigan Railway 0–6–0ST	1331
GWR Collett 0–4–2T	1412, 1417, 1432, 1459, 5806
GWR 0–6–0T	2032, 2054, 2068, 2075
GWR Collett Goods 0–6–0	2201, 2210, 2244, 2255, 3202, 3208
GWR Dean Goods 0–6–0	2327, 2354, 2382, 2386, 2449, 2452, 2482, 2483, 2516, 2543, 2556
GWR Collett 0–6–0PT	7405, 7410
GWR 'Manor' class 4–6–0	7807 *Compton Manor*
	7808 *Cookham Manor*
	7819 *Hinton Manor*
GWR Collett 2–6–2T	8103
GWR 'Dukedog' 4–4–0	9001, 9003, 9016, 9020, 9022, 9026, 9028
GWR 'Duke of Cornwall' 4–4–0	9065
TOTAL 58	

On the Oswestry to Welshpool and Newtown line of the Cambrian, the first stop was at Llynclys, followed by Pant station, pictured here in GWR days. A local train crosses the level-crossing, guarded by a small Cambrian Railways signal-cabin as it enters the station, which is devoid of passengers. This pretty little station was provided with a goods siding which closed on 6 July 1964. Passenger services lasted only a little longer, being withdrawn on 18 January 1965.

The next station along the line was at Llanymynech, seen here in GWR days. Llanymynech was at the junction of the branch to Llanfyllin. This little branch was quite substantial, and was very busy during the construction of the Lake Vyrnwy reservoir in the 1880s. It survived until the mid-1960s, closing to freight in 1964 and to passengers in 1965.

Another view of Llanymynech station, showing part of the main station building, the rather elegant iron footbridge and the back of the wooden waiting shelter with its Bovril advertisement. The platform is shared here with Colonel Stephens' private Shropshire and Montgomeryshire Railway.

Llanymynech station near the end of its life, with an ex-LMS 2–6–2 tank locomotive bringing in a local train. The station nameboard announces that here is the junction for Llanfyllin and Lake Vyrnwy. The station closed to passengers on 18 January 1965 and to goods on 6 July 1964.

Frankton station on the Cambrian line from Oswestry to Whitchurch. This single platform station with a rather grand building was reached after the line crossed the Shrewsbury and Chester Railway at Whittington (High Level), which closed in 1960. Frankton station lasted little longer, closing in 1965.

The platforms at Ellesmere station as they appeared in GWR days. The station appears busy with freight traffic, with a locomotive shunting on the main line. The stationmaster in the 1960s was a Mr Jones, now resident in Penmaenmawr, on the north Wales coast.

The substantial and handsome exterior of the main station building at Ellesmere station, 1940s. Passengers can be seen deep in discussion at the entrance and what looks like an old Austin Seven motor car is parked close by. The station closed to passengers on 18 January 1965 and to goods on 28 March of the same year. The station became a junction when the Wrexham Central line opened in 1895. The station building still exists and is now used as offices.

The main station building at Whitchurch, the point where the Cambrian line from Oswestry met the LNWR line from Crewe to Shrewsbury.

Whitchurch station, terminus of the Cambrian line from Oswestry, 1950s. The station was provided with substantial goods facilities, being the freight exchange point between the LNWR/LMS and Cambrian/GWR.

Another view of Whitchurch station, showing the signal-box and main station building. The Cambrian route from Oswestry closed in 1965 and the station ceased to be a junction, although it remains open, serving trains operating over the old LNWR route between Crewe and Shrewsbury.

THE JOINT LINES

Church Stretton. Railway Station

The very attractive original station at Church Stretton on the joint LNWR/GWR Shrewsbury–Hereford line. This picture would have been taken at the turn of the century and there are metal advertisements on the wall and overbridge for such things as Pears soap, Players Navy Cut cigarettes, and Allsopps ale.

The Shrewsbury and Hereford Railway was incorporated in 1846 and opened in 1849. The line was taken over jointly by the LNWR and GWR in 1854. Given that both companies had been involved in some extremely nasty disputes when Captain Mark Huish had been Managing Director of the LNWR this joint ownership must have brought about some strained relationships between Euston and Paddington in the early years of joint operations. The first station on the line, after leaving Shrewsbury, was Condover (closed to passengers on 9 June 1958 and to goods on 7 October 1963), followed by Dorrington. The station at Dorrington is pictured here prior to the Second World War with an unidentified LMS Stanier 'Black Five' 4–6–0 drawing in to the platform with a train for the Central Wales line to Swansea. A couple of members of the station staff are awaiting arrival of the train and milk churns sit on the platform, probably ready to be loaded on to this train. Like the station at Condover, Dorrington closed to passengers on 9 June 1958 and to goods on 15 March 1965.

A typical Great Western station at Church Stretton. This structure replaced the original station, which was closed on 23 May 1914. The station was provided with goods facilities and these were closed on 19 September 1966. The station itself still remains in use. This picture seems to have been taken in the 1930s, judging by the advertisements on the station fence for such products as Pears soap. In the distance, shunting is going on in the goods yard.

The tiny Wistanstow Halt, which lay between Church Stretton and Craven Arms, after the line had passed through Little Stretton and Marsh Brook. All of these Halts were closed in June 1958.

After leaving Wistanstow Halt, the line passed through Craven Arms & Stokesay station (closed to goods on 6 May 1968) and then entered Onibury station, pictured here, looking towards the level-crossing, in the 1930s. This attractive little station was closed on 9 June 1958.

The long platforms at Ludlow station, 1950s. Ludlow was reached after the line had passed through Bromfield (closed to passengers in 1958 and to goods in 1964). In the centre background is the goods shed.

The platform and main station building at Ludlow as it appeared in the years before the First World War. On the extreme left is the station bookstall, probably owned by W.H. Smith, as most station bookshops were in those days, and several advertisements cover the entrance to the tunnel, on the right, one of which is for Oxo, a product still very much with us. Several passengers await a train, which appears to be due. Ludlow is a major tourist centre, many people coming here to view the town and its castle. Ludlow was also a junction for the goods-only line serving quarries at Bitterley and Clee Hill. The station was also provided with substantial goods facilities, which were closed on 6 May 1968. The station itself remains open, serving as it does such an important tourist destination. The Shrewsbury and Hereford line is still important, connecting Shrewsbury with Hereford and Worcester. Steam excursions sometimes operate over the line, between Chester and Hereford.

Abdon Clee Stone Quarry Works.

At the end of the goods-only branch from Ludlow lay the Abdon Clee stone quarry, seen here in the early 1950s. The quarry company's own diesel locomotive hauls wagons away from the stone hopper after loading. The little branch closed to traffic on 7 November 1960.

The railway yard at Bitterley quarry, situated about halfway along the branch from Ludlow. In the background is a rake of little stone wagons from the quarry face, while a rake of stone-filled main line wagons belonging to the Clee Hill DHU Stone Co. await departure from the quarry.

The substantial goods yard of the Bitterley quarry in the 1930s. In the background are the stone-crushing mills and wagon-loading facilities, and heaps of crushed stone can be seen on the right. On the extreme right are the little tipper wagons, some full of stone, along with empties, which were used to remove stone from the quarry face. There is also a horse in view, used to haul these little wagons to and from the face itself. Several main line wagons are in the yard, those on the left being already full and awaiting a locomotive to collect them for onward distribution to destinations on the main line system. In the centre of the picture, several plank wagons and hopper wagons, many belonging to the GWR, are waiting to be loaded with stone products from the quarry. A horse-drawn rake of little quarry tipper wagons is coming towards the main yard.

Minsterley Railway Station and Steam Saw Mills.

From Shrewsbury, another joint line ran from a junction with Upton Magna to join the Cambrian line from Oswestry to Welshpool at Buttington. Between Hanwood and Yockleton there was a branch to Minsterley, with intermediate stations named Plealey Road and Pontesbury. Here, the terminus station at Minsterley can be seen in a rather rural setting, with the Steam Saw Mills beyond. All three stations along the branch were closed to passengers on 5 February 1951 but survived for freight traffic into the 1960s. Plealey Road closed to goods on 31 December 1962, Pontesbury closed to goods on 15 March 1965 and Minsterley survived the longest, not closing to goods traffic until 1 May 1967. The little branch was then closed altogether.

The first station on the joint line from Upton Magna to Buttington was Hanwood, followed by Yockleton. The single line station, with rather substantial main station building, is seen here in pre-First World War days, complete with staff, one of whom has a wife, two daughters and a new baby. Several milk churns litter the platform, and the usual Pears soap advertisement is attached to the fence.

An ex-Lancashire and Yorkshire Railway Aspinall 0–6–0 no. 12141 arrives at Yockleton station with a local train in the 1930s. The station, along with Hanwood, closed on 12 September 1960.

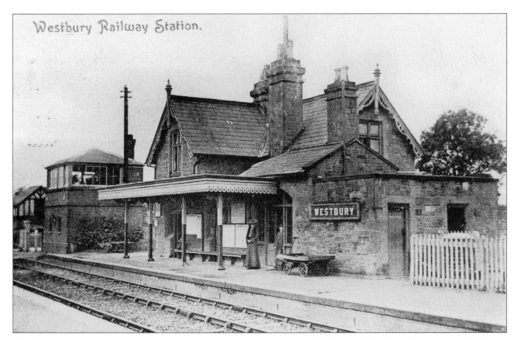

The large, stone-built station at Westbury with its unusual signal-cabin in the Edwardian period, judging by the dress and hat worn by the solitary passenger awaiting a train here. Westbury station was a passing point and so was provided with two platforms.

Westbury station in BR days, showing the main building and level-crossing. Westbury was provided with goods facilities, which were closed on 15 March 1965. The station itself, along with the final two on the line, at Plas-y-Court and Brieden, was closed to passengers on 12 September 1960. The whole line was closed in 1965.

LNWR ROUTES

Bucknell station on the LNWR Central Wales line, which left the joint Shrewsbury–Hereford line at Craven Arms. Here, a little LNWR tank locomotive brings a train into the station, which is the last in Shropshire before the line enters mid-Wales.

A non-stop train enters Broome station headed by an LNWR tank locomotive at the turn of the century. At that time, the station was provided with only simple wooden station buildings and wooden platforms. Broome is the first station on the Central Wales line from Craven Arms. This LNWR line gave the Euston company access to south Wales, right into the heart of its old enemy the GWR, and ran across country from Craven Arms, via Builth Wells, where it met the Cambrian line from Moat Lane Junction to Talyllyn Junction, to Llandovery. From there the line ran over GWR metals to Pontardulais, and on to Swansea over its own tracks. The line was scheduled for complete closure in 1963, but protests from passengers forced BR to think again and it remains open to passengers only, now reaching Swansea over ex-GWR metals, via Llanelli. The line continues to fight for its survival, with only a sparse service operated by single-coach 'Sprinter' units. With the coming of railway privatization, the line appears to be under an ever increasing threat, although railway-users' organizations will continue to fight for its retention. It remains to be seen whether the fight will be successful, and the Central Wales line will survive into the new century.

The wooden signal-box and main station building at Broome in LNWR days. Also appearing in the photograph are the station staff and a passenger.

Passengers leaving Broome station in LMS days. Note the fashions of the day and the motor cars in the background. On the extreme right of the picture are the goods shed and yard.

Bucknell station in LNWR days, with one of the company's locomotives approaching the station at the head of a mixed goods train. The view is from the level-crossing and shows the attractive stone-built main building on the left, and the simple wooden waiting room on the right.

Bucknell station, looking towards the level-crossing. In the background is the LNWR signal-box and home starting signal, while on the right is the goods yard and shed complete with wagons. The station staff, one of whom is a young boy, are posed on the platform.

The platform, staff and local policeman at Bucknell station with LNWR 'Lady of the Lake' class locomotive, seen here as *Engineer South Wales*. The engine was originally built in 1852 as no. 135 *Bat*, renumbered 1135 in 1862, and renamed *Locomotion* in 1887. The locomotive survived in departmental use into the twentieth century, not being scrapped until 1920.

Bucknell station in LMS days, with the 'target' style nameboard on the extreme left. A train is seen approaching the main platform after traversing the level-crossing. The station remains open for passengers only.

Prees station, on the LNWR Shrewsbury–Crewe line, in LMS days. The LNWR developed this line when local interests in mid-Wales began promoting a line between Shrewsbury and the coast, a plan supported financially by the Euston company. The LNWR felt that the S&CR would provide a through route which would link south Wales with Lancashire as opposed to Cheshire. The line was authorized in 1853, but it was not allowed to enter the joint Shrewsbury station for several years, terminating instead in a field more than a mile away.

Ex-LMS Stanier 8F 2–8–0 no. 48418 passes through Prees station at the head of a goods train in BR days. The station remains open but lost its goods facilities from 6 October 1969.

Hadnall station, on the Shrewsbury–Crewe line, in LNWR days. Locomotives which had been newly built or had been under heavy repair would often run in rakes of four from Crewe to Hadnall, where they would terminate. They would then be lined up in the siding, behind the main station building on the left of this photograph, and then return to Crewe, tender-first.

Hadnall station in LMS days, with a 'Black Five' 4–6–0 at the head of a passenger train entering the station. In the background, several private owner wagons are in the siding. Unlike other stations on the route, Hadnall station was closed in the mid-1960s.

Although this picture is not of the best quality, it shows a rare view of the ex-LNWR locoshed at Whitchurch. The shed was a sub of Crewe North (code 5A in BR days) and, in January 1954, had an allocation of three ex-LMS class 2P 4–4–0 locomotives, along with one from Oswestry shed (89A) for use on the ex-Cambrian line. The locomotive in the shed yard, an ex-GWR Collett double-framed 'Dukedog' no. 9020, is the Oswestry-based engine. The shed was closed in 1964 and later demolished.

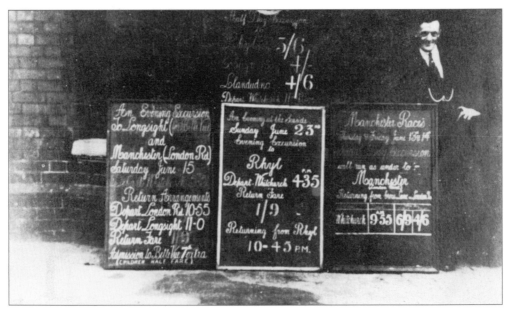

The booking office at Whitchurch station in 1935, with the booking clerk standing behind chalk-written advertisements for LMS excursions to places like Rhyl, on the north Wales coast, for a fare of 1s 9d, and Manchester races.

Another picture of less than perfect quality, but worth inclusion because it shows a brand-new 'Princess-Coronation Pacific on running-in trials over the route from Crewe to Shrewsbury.

Ex-LMS Stanier 8F 2–8–0 no. 48110 passes through Whitchurch station from Shrewsbury to Crewe in 1953.

Trench Crossing station, on the LNWR line from Stafford to Wellington. The line was on the Shropshire Union Railways and Canal Company's route, which included this line and a half share in the line between Wellington and Shrewsbury. The line from Stafford to Wellington was engineered by George Lee and no major works were required. While in dispute with the Shrewsbury and Birmingham Railway, the LNWR developed its route from Stafford, especially at its approach to Wellington, where industry was fast developing. The line had six intermediate stations – Trench Crossing, pictured here, Oakengates (Market Street), Newport, the most important, Donnington, Gnosall and Hadley. There was little traffic along the route and local trains did not stop at all stations. As a through route to Shrewsbury from Stafford, the line survived until closure in 1964. Hadley was a junction with the LNWR line to Coalport, which closed to passengers in June 1952 and to freight in December 1960.

The exterior of the LNWR station at Coalport. The station was the terminus of the branch from Wellington, with stations at Hadley, Oakengates, Matins Lee, Stirchley and Madeley Market. Services were sparse, and the line closed in 1960.

WEM

*An early 1960s view of Wem station exterior, on the ex-LNWR line between Shrewsbury and Whitchurch,
for access to Crewe. This line was opened in 1858. The photographs in this section are from a private family
album and are not quite as good as those produced professionally, but along with other material they form a
complete record of this wayside station.*

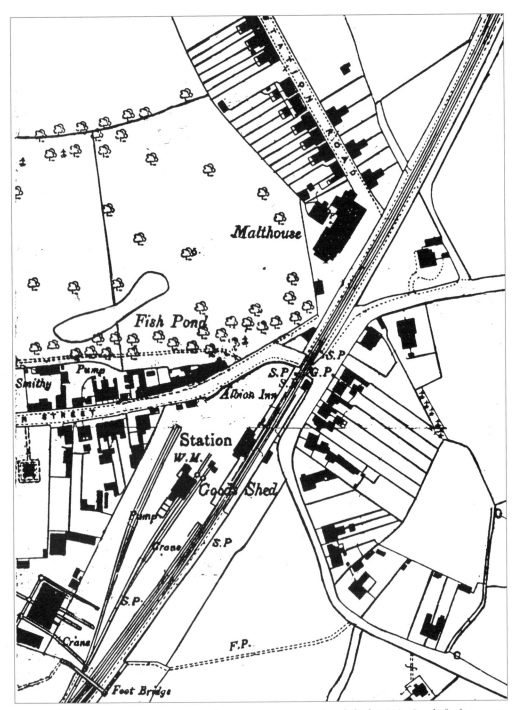

A plan of Wem station, showing the main line, station, goods yard and shed, 1902. Goods facilities were provided when the station opened, but were closed from 8 April 1971.

A distant view of Wem station, showing the covered LNWR footbridge linking the platforms, 1960s. Before the line from Shrewsbury to Crewe was authorized, three proposals were put forward for branch lines to Wem in 1845. The first plan, lodged in November 1845, was for the Shrewsbury and Wem Railway, which was designed to 'form, in conjunction with the Shropshire Union and other railways, the most direct communication between Bristol, Swansea, and South Wales, and Manchester, Liverpool, Birkenhead, the North of England, and Scotland, being the connecting link of only ten miles between the Hereford and Shrewsbury Railway and the Shropshire Union at Wem' (local press report). Several banks were involved in financing this plan, including the London Joint Stock Bank, the National Provincial Bank, Messrs Adams, Adams, Warren & Co., the North and South Wales Bank, the Whitchurch & Ellesmere Banking Co., and Messrs Rock, Eyton & Co. The chief engineer for this proposed route was to be Samuel Clegg. Other proposals put forward at the same time included a branch to Wem from the Shropshire Union Railway at Bettisfield, and a branch to Wem from the Shrewsbury, Oswestry and Chester Junction Railway from Leaton. All proposals planned to have their station near the junction of Ellesmere Road and Lowe Hill. None of these proposals actually came to fruition, although the Shrewsbury and Wem formed the basis of the LNWR line to Crewe.

The exterior of Wem station, early 1960s. The LNWR line was authorized in 1853, and by March 1858 the section near Wem was nearing completion, as *Eddowes Journal* reported: 'We are glad to find that this important link of railway communication is fast approaching completion. Yesterday the residents on the old line of road between Shrewsbury and Wem were astonished with the sight of a railway engine passing upon a truck, drawn by twenty one fine horses, which was safely landed by the engineering skill of Mr Edward Jeffreys on the rails, at the eight mile bridge, two miles from Wem, and in the course of a few days the inhabitants of that district will see the iron horse snorting his way along the newly created road. We understand that the foundation stones of the stations will be laid this day at Whitchurch, and on Thursday at Wem.' These were very exciting times.

The very first timetable for the Shrewsbury–Crewe railway, published 1 September 1858.

A view of Aston Road, Wem, looking towards the station, 1920. The view is interesting because the station has yet to be provided with a footbridge. The footbridge was provided in 1923, at the time that the station platforms were raised, making such provision necessary.

An LMS advertisement for a day excursion to New Brighton, 1934. The fare was 6s from Wem.

A horse and cart display advertising LMS services outside Wem station, *c.* 1931. On display are picture posters for Southport and Blackpool, which would be collectors' items today, along with an advertisement for an excursion to see Blackpool Illuminations for 5*s* 6*d* (27½p). The carter at this time was Harry Prince.

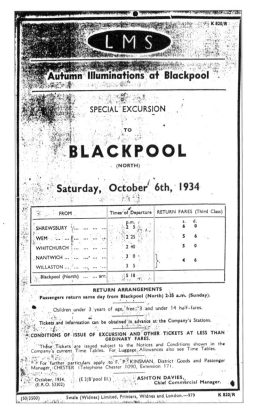

An LMS advertisement for an excursion to Blackpool Illuminations, 6 October 1934. The fare from Wem was still 5*s* 6*d*.

Wem station, complete with flower beds, a familiar sight on many wayside stations at this time, and an ex-LMS 'Black Five' 4–6–0 in the goods yard, early 1950s. The first railway accident at Wem occurred in March 1863, as reported in the *Shrewsbury Chronicle*: 'On Wednesday last, an old man of 74, named James Walters, met his death under the following circumstances: As the train which leaves Salop at 5.15 was proceeding at about 28 or 30 miles an hour, between Wem and Prees, deceased was seen by the engine driver standing on the six foot apparently engaged, with others, in gathering the hay on the slopes. On seeing the train approach, he stooped down to pick up his hat, which was lying against the rails, when he was struck down by the life guard on the axle box of the engine on the six foot. As soon as the driver saw him step towards the train, he blew the whistle and shut off steam, but could not possibly have prevented the accident. The old man died on Thursday, and on Saturday an inquest was held at the White Lion Inn, Wem, when the above facts were deposed to. Mr Walmsley, surgeon of Wem, stated that death was caused by concussion of the brain, produced by a blow from some blunt instrument. Verdict, "Accidental death".'

Wem station, with Mrs Sherwood and her dog, Megan, on the platform, February 1982.

Wem station platform, showing the LNWR footbridge and signal-cabin, 1964. In this view are, from left to right, John Butters, Mrs Crocker and Bill Thorley.

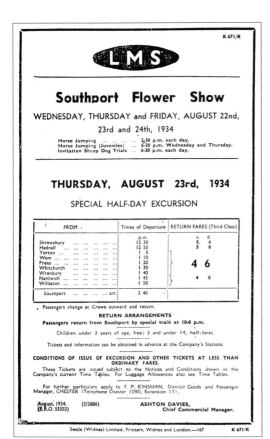

An LMS advertisement for excursions to the Southport Flower Show, August 1934. The fare from Wem was 4s 6d.

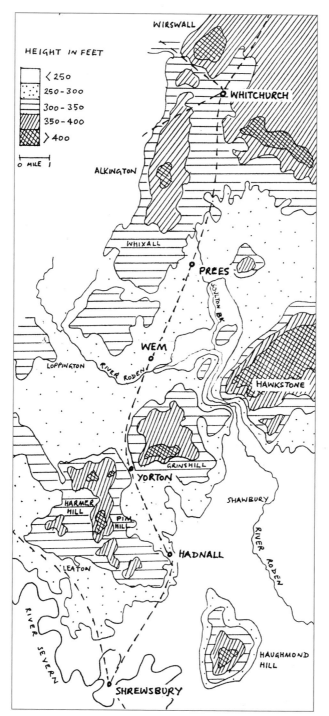

A relief map of the route of the railway between Shrewsbury and Whitchurch, via Wem. All stations, except Hadnall, are still in existence. Goods facilities, however, have ceased to exist at these stations. Prees lost its goods sidings on 6 October 1969 and Yorton's went on 6 April 1964.

Mrs Sherwood and her dog, Megan, pose for this photograph on a station seat at Wem, February 1982. Behind her are BR advertisements for £9 London Saver tickets and for Family Railcards.

Mrs Sherwood and Megan on Wem station platform, February 1982.

An LMS advertisement for cheap tickets to Wem for the cycle carnival, 4 September 1935. The advertisement states that first and third class tickets can be bought at single fare for the return journey. It also states that the 1.15 p.m. train from Crewe to Whitchurch will be extended to Wem on that date. A special return train, at 11.12 p.m., would also run, calling at all stations to Crewe. This was a very important event at Wem in those days.

Station staff at Wem at the station entrance, early 1960s. Left to right: -?-, Aubrey Chidlow and Jim Birch.

Staff on the station platform at Wem with carts full of milk churns. Behind the fence was a wooden platform specially provided for collection and delivery of milk churns. A gate in the fence gave access to the platform. This wooden platform was still in existence in the 1950s and was a good vantage point for train spotting.

Wem station staff, 1950s. Back row, left to right: Harry Gregory and Aubrey Chidlow; front row: Bill Prince, Reg Parsons, Gerry Morris and David Cheshire.

Wem station staff, mid-1960s. Left to right: Jim Birch, George Smith, Aubrey Chidlow, -?-.

Wem station staff, *c.* 1930. Left to right: Harry Stephens, Tim Carswell, Owen Lewis and Harry Gregory.

The last stationmaster at Wem was John Bishop, seen here in 1965.

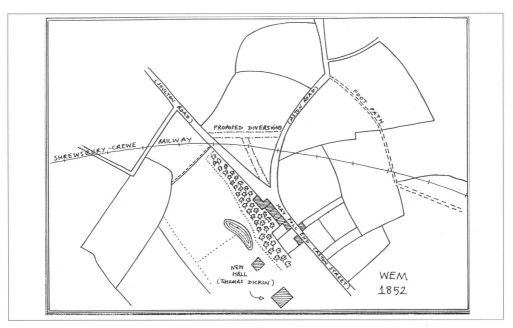

A map of Wem showing the route of the Shrewsbury–Crewe Railway and road diversions needed to accommodate the new line, 1852.

Wem station platform, with LNWR passenger train, 1910. This shows the platforms before they were raised in 1923 and the footbridge was added. Fare dodging was not unknown on the railway, as this report from *Eddowes Journal*, 19 November 1879 shows: 'Police Court, Thursday, before Captain Dicken and Sir W.M. Honeyman, Bart. Travelling Without a Ticket: J. Rogers alias J. Jarvis, a betting man, was charged with travelling from Edge Hill, Liverpool, to Wem in a third class carriage. Defendant pleaded guilty, and said he thought of meeting with his master at Edge Hill. This, he failing to do, he had taken his ticket from Liverpool to Edge Hill. Thomas Thurston, a detective in the employ of the London and North Western Railway Company, said on Tuesday, the 11 November, when examining tickets at Wem, the prisoner was found under the seat in a third class carriage. It was with difficulty that he was removed, and he (witness) was instructed to press the charge. Fined £5, including costs, or one month's hard labour.'

Wem sidings, 1930s. A horse and cart is being loaded with sugar-beet for Allscott.

L. M. & S. R.

Wem

An LMS luggage label for Wem station.

A view of the railway sidings at Wem station at the turn of the century, taken from the Bridgefields footbridge. Isherwood's timber yard is on the left, and Kynaston's maltings (1897) can be seen in the distance.

An invoice from Albert Isherwood & Co., Railway Sawmills, Wem, dated 2 November 1963 for £1 10s 0d. The sidings would be gone from Wem by 1971.

A winter view of the railway and station at Wem, showing the Isherwood timber yard and saw mills.

Another winter view of the railway at Wem.

Wem station from a nearby bridge showing the sawmills, mid-1960s. In the sidings are coal wagons belonging to the Wem Coal Company.

Phone : WEM 78   19/1/61   19

MRS Sherwood

Bought of   THE WEM COAL CO.

Take notice that you are to receive .... cwts of coal in .... sacks, each containing 1-cwt.

Tons	Description	Price	£	s.	d.
5	Non 74	8/10	2	4	2

Carter .....G.F.....   Received by ....

A receipt for coal purchased from the Wem Coal Company on 19 January 1961.

Wem station and many of its buildings were demolished in the 1960s, but some buildings did survive, including the goods shed, pictured here.

Another view of the goods shed, with assorted rubbish outside. All of the major stations on the Shrewsbury–Crewe line, including Nantwich, Whitchurch and Wem, were built using Staffordshire blue bricks. The remainder of the stations on the route were of red brick construction.

The gangers' hut at Wem as it appeared in July 1986.

The Wem station handcart lying abandoned in the goods shed.

Ex-LMS 'Black Five' 4–6–0 no. 45097 is seen here at Wem station, late 1950s.

Ex-LMS Stanier 'Princess-Coronation' Pacific no. 46235 *City of Birmingham* is leaving Wem station with a local train, the engine being run-in after major overhaul at Crewe works. This particular locomotive is now preserved at Birmingham Museum of Science and Industry, having been presented to the city after her withdrawal by BR. This view was taken *c.* 1960.

An unidentified ex-LMS Stanier 8F 2–8–0 approaches Wem from Shrewsbury, 1965. In the background is Isherwood's nursery and beyond that is Wem mill.

A BR 'Standard' class 2–6–0 enters Wem station on shunting duty, 1965.

An artist's impression of the previous train at Wem station.

The rebuilt Wem station, looking north, 14 June 1986. The grand old station buildings have been replaced by simple brick-built waiting rooms and steam trains have been replaced by DMU trains for local traffic. The station was threatened with closure in the 1960s under Beeching's proposals, but many objectors forced BR to think again and the station remains open today.

A DMU train draws into Wem station in 1963, before its bridge and station buildings were demolished. In the background, Aubrey Chidlow is acting as porter.

A DMU in West Midlands Passenger Transport Executive markings enters Wem station, mid-1980s. Nowadays, class 150 'Sprinters' operate trains along the Shrewsbury–Crewe line, many running through to Cardiff.

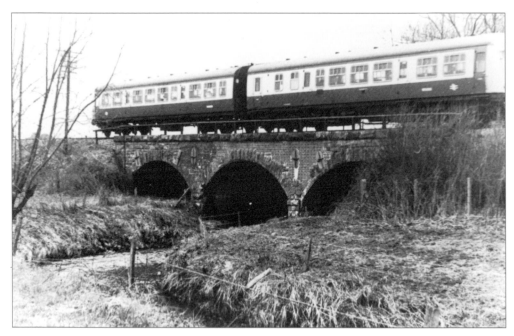

A Crewe to Shrewsbury DMU train crosses the river Roden at Wem, February 1982. This bridge actually collapsed early in 1858. Fortunately, this was before trains actually ran over the line.

An unidentified BR Brush Type 4 (class 47) Co-Co locomotive runs through Wem station, July 1986. These diesel-electric locomotives, built to replace steam traction, are now themselves disappearing from Britain's railway system, many having been withdrawn in recent years.

OTHER RAILWAYS

Pipe Gate station, on the North Staffordshire Railway (NSR) line from Silverdale (where a link to Stoke-on-Trent could be made) to Market Drayton, authorized in 1864. The LNWR was asked to become involved in the construction of this route, but declined, and the NSR built it alone.

Another view of Pipe Gate station in NSR days. Passenger services on the line to Market Drayton were withdrawn in 1956, the station closing to such traffic on 7 May of that year. Pipe Gate survived for goods traffic until 1 February 1963.

Another station on the NSR route to Market Drayton was Burwarton, seen here before the 1923 'Grouping'.

Another railway operating in Shropshire was the Bishop's Castle Railway, built in 1866 to join the Shrewsbury and Hereford Joint Railway, with the prospect of reaching mid-Wales. This view shows the exterior of the line's terminus at Bishop's Castle station, with its goods shed on the extreme left and the back of its main building just in front.

The platform at Bishop's Castle station with one of the railway's passenger trains awaiting departure. Station staff and passengers are on the platform, along with a barrow and various goods. From Bishop's Castle, there were stations at Lydham Heath, Eaton, Plowden and Hordeley. The line's other terminus was at Craven Arms and Stokesay.

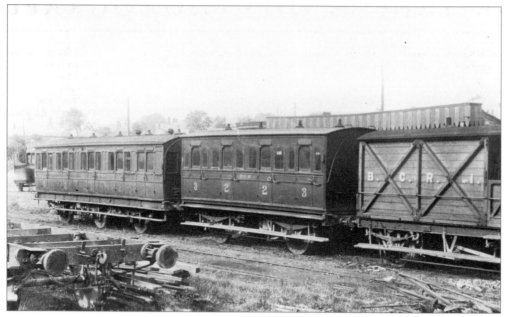

Bishop's Castle station, September 1928. A train of two coaches, both mixed third and second class, with a goods brake van behind. This little railway became more and more decrepit over the years and finally closed down on 30 April 1935.

ACKNOWLEDGEMENTS

We would like to record our grateful thanks to all who assisted us in putting this project together; their efforts on our behalf have been invaluable.

Special thanks must go to Dr Ken Sherwood of Nene College, Northampton, for providing all of the material on Wem and its station, and to Sheila E. Hart BA of Shrewsbury, who provided many rare views of the railways in Shropshire.

Others who have given invaluable assistance have been Peter Owen, Gwyn Roberts and Lens of Sutton.

Our thanks also go to Alwen and Sheila for their continued support.

BRITAIN IN OLD PHOTOGRAPHS

To order any of these titles please telephone our distributor, Littlehampton Book Services on 01903 721596
For a catalogue of these and our other titles please ring Regina Schinner on 01453 731114